AF577255

Aegean Doorway

Miriam Sagan

Zephyr Press
1984

First edition.
Printed in the United States of America.

Some of these poems appeared in: *Cottonwood Review*, *Croton Review*, *Earth First*, *Gusto*, *Hanging Loose*, *Indiana Review*, *Pinchpenny*, *Plainswoman*, *Poets On*, *Salome*, *Star Line*, and *West Branch*.

Design by Ed Hogan.

I would like to thank the MacDowell Colony, the Virginia Center for the Creative Arts, and the Briarcombe Foundation, where some of these poems were written.

Publication of this book was assisted by a grant from the Massachusetts Council on the Arts and Humanities.

ISBN 0-939010-05-4
Library of Congress Catalogue Card No. 83-91403

ZEPHYR PRESS
13 Robinson Street
Somerville, Massachusetts 02145

Aegean Doorway

Atlantis

The women walk naked
Down alabaster steps
Into the warm mineral bath.
Steam rises as a woman
With painted nails and heavy rings
Tells us her dream
Of soldiers and a lost bracelet.

Bright flags are strung across the pool.
I swim the breast stroke
And steer by the painted line
On the bottom, thinking
Of pearl divers
And a fresh water spring
From the ocean floor.

Swimmer above the sunken city:
Submerged spires
And coral domes,
My nipples harden to water's touch.
But once on land again, the mermaid
Changes her tail for legs:
Each step is a knife.

I take my dress from the hook.
The city in a cold wind
Seems safe
In its idea of the future
As if no wave will rise.
At home, I look up "Atlantis"
In the encyclopedia:

Island in an archipelago
Just beyond the Pillars of Hercules.
All our maps show it
In the western sea: Fortunate Isles,
Isle of Seven Cities, Atalantis, Atlantica,
Object of voyages of discovery,
Called Avalon, Green Island, America.

Web

I open the window to look at the moon
And there, in a corner,
A spider's web outlined in dew:
Enormous. Perfect. Shimmering.

You take my hand as if to kiss
Or sink your teeth into the palm
But instead lift it to your face
To touch the drops condensed on your beard.

To Saint Catherine

Catherine, you are the patron saint
Of unmarried women over twenty-six;
So let me sparkle, flare, and flame
Like the firework that rotates in your name;
And let me sit in calm repose:
Stained glass window of the rose;
And let me spring like cartwheel, sprung
By a girl in the park in springtime;
And let me hold the wheel like Fortune,
And let my body break that wheel.

The Animal Husband

For a long time, unmarried, I
Kept to clean sheets, my own blood,
Kept to daylight, where men remain men,
Slept alone.

Then you arrived, with berries and cream,
Wooing with mushrooms, roots in a human form,
And I married you,
Dark beard and chest of fur.

And you become a badger
Clever, sleepy, fierce,
The earth your house
We burrow deep.

By air you are raven,
The wise thief,
Stealing a bright ring
Or a piece of meat.

I remain a woman, so I think
But you call me raccoon
Washing in the stream
Giving you a bite and a kiss.

The Princess and Curdie

after George MacDonald

Safe in bed on the floor
In a valley of the city,
You read the fairy book aloud:
"A mountain is a strange and awful thing,
Heart of the earth escaped
From the dungeon, heart not of blood but
Buried sunlight that keeps the earth alive."
I put my lips to your ear, kiss:
When the door is opened
Floor falls away, beneath our feet
An abyss, starless,
And a moon shining inside the room
Spinning like an enormous wheel.
After love, we return and sit naked.
You take my photograph,
Hand me a cup of chocolate, and tell
My fortune with cards and stars.
"Shapes are only dresses,
And dresses are only names."
The room smells faintly of burning roses.
At breakfast we tell the dream of earthquakes
Recurring throughout this neighborhood.
A crystal breaks light, scatters rainbows.
The book ends: "One day at noon
The whole city fell with a roaring crash,
Cries of men, shrieks of women,
Then a great silence."
We kiss good-bye and I walk out
Into the street. I want
To gaze into an emerald, magic,
To see if you are safe.

The Secret Garden

The rose garden buried in snow.
Stone baskets of fruit flank the door.
The tapestry comes alive by moonlight.

We climb the castle steps,
Barefoot, in our white nightgowns.

Our mother in her fur hat and cape
Rides away all winter on a train.
In this story, we feed ourselves.

Little sister, playing orphan,
You are my charm of bread and milk.

The princess is homesick in the attic
Until the bare garret suddenly transformed
By colored lanterns, Persian rugs.

A thorn pricks the palm,
A blood stain on the sheet,

A mole appears under one breast:
Punctuation, a portent,
New star in the known sky.

A formal pattern of paths and fountains
Set as a grid against the landscape.

The key buried,
The rose garden walled,
The only one we want to enter.

Zazen Suite

From all over the city we come
Running, on buses, the streetcars
In our accustomed clothes
Enter by the side door
And take off our shoes
One two three four five six seven eight nine ten
In the clear light of Haight Street
As in the clearlight of desire
A man threw a bright orange at me, said
Are you responsible for this weather?
1 2 3 4 5 6 7 8 9 10
Crossing the Dolores like crossing a dream
With a green line of palms down the middle
You ask: who kissed and bruised your neck,
A man or a woman?
Much later, we take a taxi home in the rain;
The driver says: is that Venus, the evening star.
I come in and take off my shoes
I bow to the cushion
I bow to you
I bow to the first glimpse of the sea
Seen between green hills beyond ravine.
Leg bad, right leg cramped, asleep, pins and needles,
Left leg not in present time.
One two three four five six seven eight nine ten
Last night the moon was full
All nine planets aligned in the sky
I filled up two containers of water
In case of earthquake
You serve black tea and red honey
In small chipped Japanese cups
Black characters on white
1 2 3 4 5 6 7 8 9 10

The girl at the check-out counter asks:
"Do you know any guys who are 26 and single?"
Once, when we made love with the window open
I heard a low-flying helicopter, thought
This is the end of the world.
Orange poppies
In the brilliant, green, abandoned field
White cabbage moths scattering, playing in pairs
The hall is empty before we enter
As if to dance, but instead
Sit down: zazen: the grid: music
We do not move in time
And yet
I cast a shadow on the screen
Hear the sounds of the street
Black kids on bicycles, sirens, old woman
Calling in a loud Chinese
Sudden birds
Child bouncing a basketball
1 . . . 2 . . . 3 . . . 4 . . . 5 . . . 6 . . . 7 . . . 8 . . . 9 . . . 10 . . .
These neighborhoods, innumerable, vow
To let them save me
The bell rings, such relief
Like the time I pissed behind the rock
After we were stuck on the boat for hours
In the middle of the bay
With the engine down.
I get up and put on my shoes.

South Ridge Zendo

Walking to Philip's downhill in the rain
A bird embryo on the sidewalk
Zazen organizes events around itself
Like opening or closing a green umbrella.

Tears begin when I sit with incense
Like the smell of you late last night
Hair full of smoke and earth
As you pull my pants off in bed.

Bowing together now
An unopened rosebud on the altar.
Outside in raindrops we can't stop laughing:
Did you see Philip pull that thread out of his robe?

Mindless, happy, going home I am singing
All Buddhas, ten directions, three times
I've Got A Right To Sing The Blues and
Buddy Can You Spare A Dime.

Climbing uphill, an almost full moon
Hits me like a moan in the belly
And I turn to look and *see*
White bell flowers heavy on the stem.

The Hunter

In a greyware pot
Shaped like a woman's belly
I place two purple iris
Two columbine
Two red brush clover
One California poppy.

I walk through the long grass
Carrying a broom and zafu.
In the shallow woods
I sweep dead leaves and twigs
Off the wooden deck.
Bow, sit, and cross legs.

Immediately, a brown and black dog
Appears out of the underbrush
Licks my face and kisses my nose.
The trees creep closer
In a cloud of gnats.
Mosquito bites my chin twice.

Home from hunting,
The door is unlatched.
One petal of the poppy–
Yellow tipped orange,
Dry butterfly wing–
Fallen to the floor.

After Sitting

Cross-legged on the mat, facing the wall
Zazen until the bell releases us
We cross the street to the grocery store
Buy a bread loaf, a pocketful of candy.
You give me an enormous umbrella
Of lacquered green, in Japanese paper.
It isn't raining, but it will rain.
Watch out! I'm going to kiss you on the mouth.
Sitting, right hand holds the left hand, this is
The only thing the right hand knows to do.

Autumn Equinox

Up on the roof in the wind,
Hair in my face, fog rolling in,
Freeway streaming, laundry flapping.
The wheel turns and we
Are on the wheel.
Twenty minutes ago we passed
Into the autumn equinox.
Waiting. Nothing happens.
Everyone tries not to laugh.
Then ping! Music and red cloths blown wild.
No Buddha, we bow to a flower,
The whole city,
Marked by emptiness.
I retrieve my house keys
From a geranium pot.
Coming down stairs, you show me
The incense stick bent in the wind.

Buddha Flower Birthday

We squat by the duck pond.
Across the water, children
Fly a dragon kite
With orange weather balloons
And pull a cart of flowers.
Rain off and on. We chant
An unfamiliar sutra, recite
Our favorite names of flowers:
Star acacia, California poppy,
Cherry and the blossoming plum.
In Japan, they bring offerings
Of umbrellas and shoes.

Last night I dreamed
I saw your sandal in a rain puddle.
Floating away; but you came up the hill
In a yellow slicker, wearing a newspaper hat.
To touch you is to re-invent
A language in me again
Language like breath out of the belly
An animal come in out of the dark.
Beneath our umbrellas, we sit on the bank
And the passers-by smile at us
For we are the lovers—
God and goddess this moment.

A History of Burning

Like these bodies in the flame
The mind is restless
Does not stop to rest
On the monks, cross-legged
Doused in kerosene
The body crumpling as it becomes
Beacon, Buddha, corpse
Wick at last.
In Yiddish, they called the shirtwaist strikers
Firey girls
Tired of bending for a thousand years,
Dawn to dusk, a bit of lunch in paper.
"I have no more patience for talk," she said
"I am one of those who feel and suffer these things."
And the 20,000 rise up
Waving white handkerchiefs in the air.
But the door is locked
From outside,
The tenement on fire,
Girls flame from the window
Like falling stars.
A young man hands them up,
Kisses each full on the mouth
Drops them down a thousand stories
To the sidewalk of New York.
My mother says: never
Cross a picket line.
In Pompeii, the body
Is a negative space in death,
A hole shaped human in the ash.
Hiroshima, Nagasaki,
Not corpse but shadow
Flattened to the sand
In terrible outline.

Like fire itself
The mind is restless
Cannot pause for more than an instant.
I am one of those
Who feel and suffer these things.
I have no more patience for talk.

Lunch with My Tanta Sophia

Tanta Sophia and Uncle Jacobo, en route
From Venezuela to Alaska invite me to lunch
Although we haven't met since 1965, when I
Was a little girl with a braid down my back
And my father, not a relative, was rude to them.
Jacobo, white haired, looks like my grandfather,
And Sophia is plumper, if possible,
But walks with a walker and wears fewer rings.
Tanta Sophia and Uncle Jacobo
Met via Russia Poland Palestine and Cuba
Had five children and fifteen grandchildren
Who are doctors to Latin American presidents
And divorced. They ask me why I'm not married
And invite me to Caracas to meet the young folks.
We go up in an elevator on the outside of the building
To where diners orbit like the world
And Tanta Sophia and I admire suspension bridges
        and hope
There will be no earthquake during lunch.
They send me regards from my great aunt Manya
Recently arrived in Texas from Russia, who says:
"It is not hard to get used to a land of plenty."
Like my entire family of tourists and refugees,
Factory owners and revolutionaries
Tanta Sophia and Uncle Jacobo are restless,
Build a new house, then cruise to Alaska.
There, in a glacial sea on an ice floe
A seal gives birth and licks
The blood of the placenta off her pup.
But here, in the great hotel, where walls of ivy
Cascade down twenty stories to the lobby
We kiss good-bye, my Uncle Jacobo
And Tanta Sophia who is as round and dark and plump
As continents shifting on the plates
Of the imperfect, spinning, globe of earth.

On the Sunset

1.
Afraid of the Pacific's quake,
We watch the waves' white crest.
Last night, I dreamed
A lacquered Shinto gate
Rose red out of the sea;
"Signifier is the signified,"
You say; and put your mouth down
On my cunt. The word
For orgasm in French
Is "petite morte."
You say that in L.A.
Someone was murdered on the beach
At 3 A.M. Language
Is the shape of thought itself,
Half moon breaking
Through clouds.
Sun will rise
Above the eucalyptus grove,
Light that shatters, makes
Visible the shreds of bark,
Blades of grass;
Nasturtiums flood the bank,
Golden, fallen constellations.
Mind lifts as if
You ran across the field, and I
Stood open mouthed in light as
In a kiss.

2.
Mountains rise from the sea,
Staircase in mist.
Eucalyptus shed leaves:
Scimitars of red.

Fog lifts, reveals
The golden bridge.

The continent behind us:
Patchwork fields,
Grain elevator silhouette,
Dark thresher, dark silo, dark corn.
Lights blink on, one by one,
Square frame house standing alone.

3.
Someone calls the children in,
Folds laundry out of white wind,
Roses close, pink and luminous,
All over the neighborhood.
Loneliness seeps
Like the smell of vanilla
From room to room.
A woman sits up late, alone,
Bent over the balance sheet
Of her tears. In the hallway
A couple embrace.
Women kiss and quarrel
Until the quarrel rises through the walls;
Men spread out maps
On the rug, contours
Of rivers, mountains, the reproach
Of other geographies.

4.
The cardiogram is not the heart itself,
The graph is not the beat.
High in the narrow bed, beneath the sheet,
Lifeguard on drowner, you resuscitate,

And bruise me with both thumbs
On nipple, eyelid, armpit.
Panic is the opposite of breath;
These possibilities panic us:
Had our parents never met, conceived;
Had they died in the camps of death.
We should be crying in each others' arms,
I can't stop crying the the street.
Pull the shade. Blow the candle out.
Believe me. I am innocent.

Painting

for Fran Cohen Gillespie

Nothing will stay still.
You place a grid against the flower
But the petals unfold, curl up.
You set your daughter naked
On a black velvet couch
But she grows breasts, grows modest,
Slips on her underpants and climbs off.
You cannot paint fast enough.

As a girl in the museum of art,
You were drawn to the corners
Of an annunciation, or adoration;
Wondering how an angel
Slipped the robe on over his wings;
Mesmerized by a perfect lily
In a golden vase.
Nothing moves.

Unaccompanied

The notes you razored from the score
Fall to the floor like snow.

The moonlight is knee-deep,
I'd like to fall and print
A snow angel in it.

You turn from the door:
"Whoever lives here, will be happy."

Outside, the animal tracks in snow
Form dark whole notes, unreadable music.
We do not touch.

Snow falls out of the envelope
Even as you read this.

Bolinas Impressionist

The house opens to the sea, the view
Of great rocks off shore.
Inside the still life, we
Eat an omelette, a bowl of strawberries.
And talk in the kitchen,
In the ancient conversation of women
Saying: child, solitude, my mother.
Sun sets. Against the house
Lavender flowers and geraniums
Take on luminous, deep color:
Splashes of paint
On the palette of dusk.

Off Cape Ann

Like a fin seen at eye level:
The blue sail far on the horizon.

Sunbathers open their legs.
We lie face down on the sand,

Talking of the bars, of women who want to make love
Or women slow-dancing in each others' arms.

We lick the salt from our lips,
Pack up, drive inland

To a glass house, banked in flowers.
I choose geranium out of all possible colors.

Geranium, brought from Africa;
Or, says my mother

Carried across the plains
By pioneer women in wagons.

Summer night after summer night
I lean out of a window above the city

And place a geranium on the sill, until
A grey cat jumps up, completes the scene.

Yr Bodies

1.
Walking with you beneath the palms
And unimagined eucalyptus,
Hand held tight in inarticulate hand,
You explain the universe is curved;
But if it ends, I want to know,
What comes after.
And yet we sit in the park together,
Tongues in each others' mouths,
And the envious passers-by
Imagine this is love.

2.
You hang no curtains on the windows
The light of thirteen blocks
From the ocean wakes me
From the dream of a tsunami.
Girl, or goddess descended,
A golden V marks your center
Which I do not desire
Which I desire,
Which I can possess only
With the tips of my fingers.

3.
This is not your house.
You hang your black leather jacket
On the door knob
Like a shadow
Of your body, or a cocoon
From which we emerge naked
Married belly to belly
Neither arriving nor disappearing
But alone, dressed
In our own skin.

Approximately for You

I outline the most sensitive parts
Of your body: an acupuncture chart,
Or a map of the entire city.

A woman is trapped within your bonecage,
If I kiss deeply enough her breasts
Will rise beneath your flat nipples.

Even when you sleep, she turns
Towards me, surfacing like a fish
In the rain, or something shyer.

And you dream of the sea:
A stone boat, and the rower
Rowing at last upon the sand.

Aegean Doorway

after a silkscreen by Thomas McKnight

A postcard of a painting of a doorway leading
To sky to sea to scrub and sand dunes;
A mirror on a dresser, comb and brush, a glass of water
And a white towel hung in the breeze to dry.

These objects, significant, set perfectly in place
Touched everywhere by air and the clear light.
This postcard on my window
Before lagoon and hills green beneath hawks.

You wrote on the back:
"My virtue is kindness.
My love of people, animals etc.
Your fault is that you live too far away."

I remember, sister, your story
Of turning a corridor in the museum of the Acropolis
And coming face to face, nose to nose, lip to lip
With a caryatid, removed for repairs.

You with your dark eyes and wild dark hair,
The same height as that marble girl. So close
You can kiss her, or stroke her cheek.
You both stand very still.

Untitled

The little sisters
Are dancing in the kitchen
To "I Can't Get No Satisfaction"
On the radio.
They whirl each other
Across yellow linoleum.
This is the only lit room
In the entire house.

A Revision

Like St. Ursula in her white nightgown,
Asleep in the exact center
Of that great golden city,
I am waiting
For an angel to step through the door.
Instead, I carry a white rose home in my hand
From the corner florist. Light snow;
A storm enters the inner ear.
Radiator hisses. The book lies
Face down, the passage
Marked by a broken binding.
Above the dome of the observatory
The moon develops into light.
Dusk traverses the Persian rug,
Slips from the pots of basil and aloe,
Spikey "heal-burn" on the sill.
And I am waiting
For an angel to step through the door
One foot poised lightly for landing,
A green palm in the hand,
Shattering the threshold of air.
It is as if all the clocks
In the city chimed at once, as if
Red banners ripped in the breeze
As if the sea came up to the door of the house
And blew back the curtain.

A Corresponding Weather

You write from the south
That oranges freeze on the trees
Bright fruit encased in ice.

It is so cold
Birds hail out of the sky

Oxygen masks drop into our laps
The airplane crashes into the river
And we use ice floes for rafts.

In this weather ghosts appear
On photographic plates

Of ordinary family gatherings;
They are more transparent than we,
Their clothes seem old fashioned.

A wind off the glacial lake
Stills the tinkling chandelier in the abandoned house.

You write by postscript of a frostbitten heart.
I can't open the door. Against the slot
Your letters pile like a drift of snow.

Housekeeping in the Chrysalis

Snakes shed their skins,
Even worms spin silken cocoons.
Fish crawl out of the warm seas,
Sprout legs, walk away,
And lizards itch, burst
Into wings, fly off as birds.

I give away my clothes in the street:
Chiffon petticoat, velvet-lined cape.
I sit naked on the table
Beneath "Two Views of the Female Pelvis
Drawn Actual Size," and suddenly
Remember I have a skeleton.

The X-ray is a premonition.
I check my heart for a murmur,
My cough for a rattle,
My feet for blisters,
My sputum for blood.
Scar is a seam that heals itself.

I wear my lungs
Like a pair of water wings
To keep me afloat in my breath.
I adjust the weight of my pack,
Mark my place in the book
With a schedule of departures.

Once, you touched me over and over,
Polished me like a stone in water,
Wore me down.
But now the ferry pulls from the slip
Towards open water
Among white sails and gulls.

The heart's dark machine
Works its shifts overtime.
And though my skin
Is a Jacob's coat of many colors,
I step out of this dress,
I slough it off.

Breathless

A red leaf
Slips from the pages of the book.
A tree branches inside my lungs:
Silvered like an old mirror,
A developing photograph.

You say:
"Love is impossible;
Try to live in the world."
Pumpkins sit on the front porch.
The brick town shuts tight.
Still, the water goes white
Over the falls, and persists,
Falling in darkness.

The Breath Lesson

Color the lungs blue
Because breath
Is a blue ribbon unraveling
From sky to mouth.
This is the lesson of breath:
The meaning of counting to ten
Before touch. Breathless.
Pant pant panting.
Holding this breath
Holding on
Holding down both hands
With my hands
A finger along a pulse
Of between, where the bones
Join together, articulate,
Speak in unison.
The little sword of the sternum
Poised above the heart
And the ribs:
True, false,
Floating.
I am continuous with this breath
Also, this small pink flower
In a jar on the table
And the cup of tea,
Smoke of incense, separate motes
In sunlight.
Palms up, palms down,
The gliding wrist,
I cap your hands with my hands
Release as slowly
As the end of sound
When the bell stops
And echo fades, aftermath

Ends, even then
The memory of touch.
The doorway in the dark
Is the body's exact shape.
Had we the eyes to see
Body of darkness,
Body of light,
The same.
So I scoop two shallow holes
In the sand:
One for the hipbone
And one for the shoulder blades
Lie down to sleep
By the side of the river.

Aegean Doorway *was set in 12 point Aldine Roman. It was printed on acid free paper and the binding sewn for book longevity.*

An edition of 1000 was printed by Thomson-Shore, Inc., Ann Arbor, Michigan. Twenty-five are signed and numbered by the poet.